Anonymous

Bell's Picturesque Guide to American watering Places

Coney Island and what is to be seen there

Anonymous

Bell's Picturesque Guide to American watering Places
Coney Island and what is to be seen there

ISBN/EAN: 9783337144234

Printed in Europe, USA, Canada, Australia, Japan

Cover: Foto ©Andreas Hilbeck / pixelio.de

More available books at **www.hansebooks.com**

BELL'S PICTURESQUE GUIDE

TO

AMERICAN WATERING PLACES.

CONEY ISLAND

AND WHAT IS TO BE SEEN THERE.

ILLUSTRATED.

CONTAINING A FULL DIRECTORY TO ALL THE RAILROAD DEPOTS, STEAMBOAT
LANDINGS, AMUSEMENTS, AND BUSINESS PLACES, WITH A SKETCH
MAP LOCATING EACH PLACE OF NOTE, ALSO TIME TABLES
OF ALL THE RAILROADS AND STEAMBOATS.

PRICE TEN CENTS.

C. J. MACDONALD & CO., PUBLISHERS,
148 WORTH STREET, NEW YORK.

CONTENTS.

TO THE READER.

---◦◦---

IN presenting the first of a series of GUIDES TO AMERICAN WATERING PLACES to the public, my object is not only to make the reader acquainted with the historical and picturesque features of our Summer Resorts, by the aid of pen and pencil,* but to lead the visitor step by step to all the sights worth seeing—giving general and useful information with regard to Hotels, their rates, and the routes of travel of the various Railroad and Steamboat Companies—so that a day of pleasure may not be turned into a day of toil, as it often is, for the want of a reliable Guide; thus enabling visitors to make good use of the few hours set aside for recreation. Having given you some idea of the plan of this and future Books, I will, with your permission, dear reader, accompany you to CONEY ISLAND, and while on our journey I will give you a brief history of this now famous Watering Place, and upon our arrival (if you will place yourself under my guidance for a few hours), I will introduce you to my friends, famous for their enterprise in making this once barren Island what it now is. I will take you to the various places of amusement, and will tell you what the charges are; and when the time arrives I will send you where the inner man may be best satisfied, at the most reasonable cost, for this necessary indulgence; and lastly, if you will kindly refer to my "Time-Tables," I will promise that you will not experience the discomfort of marring a day's pleasure by missing the last train or boat.

JUNE, 1879.   G. C. B.

---

*The illustrations in this Guide, except in a few instances, are reproductions of pen and ink sketches by the author, taken during June, 1879.

THE DISCOVERY OF CONEY ISLAND.

" O'er the glad waters of the dark blue sea,
Our thoughts as boundless and our souls as free;
Far as the breeze can bear the billows foam,
Survey our Empire and behold our home."—BYRON.

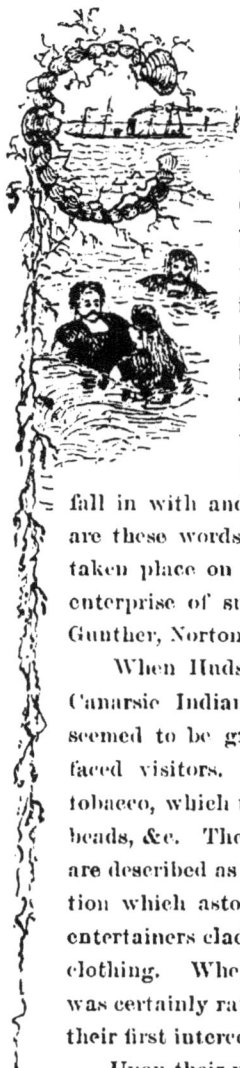

ONEY ISLAND, in the Township of Gravesend,
County of Kings, State of New York, was discovered
by that celebrated navigator, Henry Hudson (after
whom our beautiful river was named), on the morn-
ing of September 3d or 4th, 1609; and, it is stated
upon good authority, that seeing the waters swarm-
ing with fish, he sent a boat's crew to obtain some.
They landed on Coney Island, and were the first
white men that ever set foot on the soil of the
Empire State. He describes it "as a good land to
fall in with and a good land to see." How singularly appropriate
are these words when we note the remarkable changes which have
taken place on the Island within the last few years, through the
enterprise of such pioneers as Corbin, Culver, Breslin, Engeman,
Gunther, Norton and others.

When Hudson anchored off this historical strip of land, the
Canarsie Indians approached him without any hesitation, and
seemed to be gratified in making the acquaintance of their pale-
faced visitors. They brought with them deer skins and green
tobacco, which they exchanged for various articles—such as knives,
beads, &c. They were rudely clad in skins of various animals, and
are described as being very civil, exhibiting an advance in civiliza-
tion which astonished the great navigator; for, upon seeing their
entertainers clad in broadcloth, they made a request for that kind of
clothing. Whether this was supplied or not is not stated; but it
was certainly rather an unusual request for Aborigines to make on
their first intercourse with white men.

Upon their next visit some of them were dressed in mantles of
furs and feathers. They offered in barter both yellow and red copper ore,

together with ornaments and instruments made of the same metal, which Hudson's crew eagerly purchased, being under the impression that they were manufactured of gold. They also brought large quantities of maize or Indian corn, from which they made bread described as being "sweet and good." Some of the squaws brought hemp—of which they must have known the use—otherwise they would not have offered it as a present.

Hudson had remained here three days, when his peaceful intercourse with the Indians was unfortunately broken. It appears that upon a few of his men landing the second time they were immediately attacked, it is not known for what reason, but it is probable that some provocation must have been given. During the conflict John Coleman, one of the party, was pierced in the throat and instantly killed by an arrow, and two of his companions were seriously wounded. Coleman was buried upon the point of Coney Island, which Hudson, in commemoration of that sad occurrence, named Coleman's Point. It is now known as Norton's Point. This serious affray terminated their intercourse with the shore, and although the Indians again visited them as if nothing had happened, they evidently feeling that Coleman's death was a just punishment—he being the principal offender, Hudson set sail the following day, and pursued his course up the river.

This Island, whose shores are in a constant state of tumult with the boiling surf, was not, until 1873-74, a favorite resort for tourists, on account of the disreputable characters who frequented it. Now it is visited by the élite of society from all parts of the country. It is nearly surrounded by the Atlantic, affording a magnificent ocean view, and is constantly fanned by cool and refreshing breezes. It is separated from the main land by a narrow creek, and contains about sixty acres of arable land, the remainder being a singular looking mass of sand hills drifted about in wild and picturesque confusion by the action of the severe storms which often visit the Island during the Winter. It is about five miles in extent from east to west, and about one mile in width.

Having briefly referred to Coney Island of the past, we will now start on our journey of pleasure, and with that view will commence at Manhattan Beach, and by the time we arrive at the point where poor Coleman was buried the reader will have fully appreciated the beauties of the Coney Island of TO-DAY.

> " By viewing Nature, Nature's handmaid Art
> Makes mighty things from small beginnings grow,
> Thus fishes first to shipping did impart,
> Their tail the rudder and their head the prow."—DRYDEN.

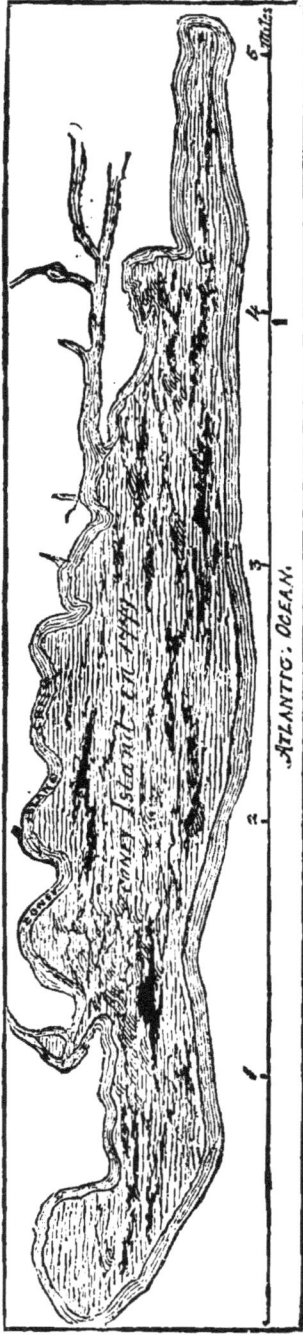

CONEY ISLAND IN 1779.

ATLANTIC OCEAN.

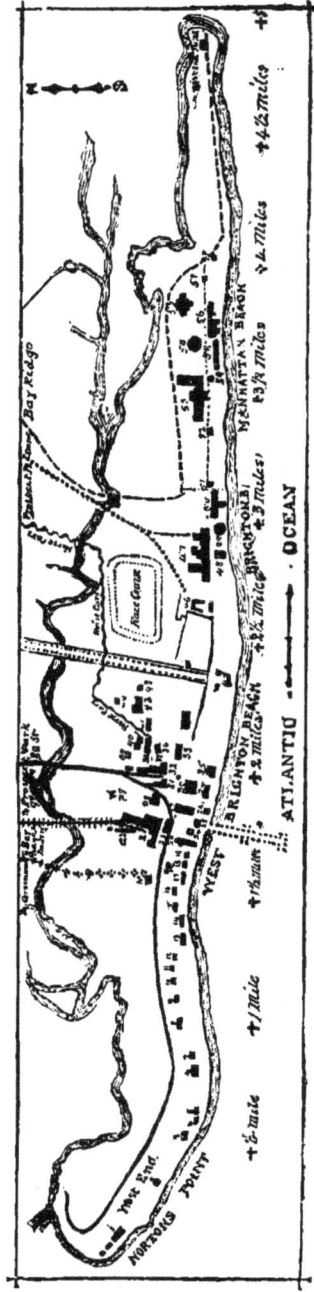

CONEY ISLAND IN 1879.

REFERENCES TO MAP, SHOWING THE DIFFERENT RAILROADS AND ROUTES OF TRAVEL.

∴ ∴ ∴ ∴ Brooklyn, Bath & Coney Island Railroad.—To Greenwood Cemetery, 5th Ave. and 27th St., Brooklyn, connecting at Locust Grove with steamers John Sylvester, Eliza Hancox and Hampden.

┼┼┼┼┼┼┼┼ New York & Sea Beach Railroad.—To Bay Ridge and Battery, New York.

━━━━━ Prospect Park & Coney Island Railroad.—To Prospect Park, 9th Ave. and 20th St., Brooklyn.

∿∿∿∿∿ Coney Island & Brooklyn Horse Cars.

• • • • • • • • • • • Brooklyn, Flatbush & Coney Island Railroad.—To Prospect Park, Bedford, Atlantic and Flatbush Avenues, Brooklyn.

– – – – – – – – – Manhattan Beach Railroad.—To Bay Ridge, Battery, Pier 8, Leroy St., 23d St., North River, also East New York, Greenpoint and 23d St., East River.

MANHATTAN BEACH HOTEL.

MANHATTAN BEACH.

►◆◄

WHEN Mr. Corbin, the President of the Manhattan Beach Improvement Company, first arranged to invest his thousands of dollars in building up this portion of the Island, how little did he imagine to what huge proportions his scheme would grow. This is now probably one of the largest and most favored Sea-side Hotels in the country, and every year new additions or wings are added to the present unique pile of buildings, in order to accommodate the enormous increase of business. Here seven hundred persons can be furnished with sleeping apartments, while the dining-rooms are capable of supplying the wants of three thousand excursionists at one sitting. Messrs. McKinnie and Burnap, the managers, are well known as caterers to the public, and their ability to supply all that is needed to any indefinite number is unquestioned.

– The Music Stand is centrally situated, and is occupied by Gilmore's Band, who will give a series of concerts every afternoon and evening, assisted by Mr. Levy, the celebrated cornet soloist, who has been engaged at an enormous salary, and will delight the lovers of music daily with some of the best pieces from his *repertoire*.

The Dancing Pavilion has long proved a source of attraction to visitors, and is so constructed that by the aid of sliding windows the happy reveler is protected from sudden showers which visit us during the heated term.

The Grand Pavilion, situated at the east end of the Hotel, will seat 1,500 persons at dining tables, one-half of which are at the service of parties bringing their lunch with them, the management having generously provided tables, seats and waiters free of charge.

The Bathing Houses are capable of furnishing room to two thousand five hundred persons, together with facilities of hot salt water baths for those who need them; and the accommodation, both as regards privacy and first-class bathing apparel, renders them unsurpassed on the American continent. Here the bather can enter the water without passing through a gaping crowd, which deters so many ladies from taking this life-giving luxury, because the bathers are protected by a neat fence which runs several feet into the water, thus separating them from spectators. Colored electric lights are used as the evening advances, and numbers avail themselves of these lights to take at night a dip, forming perhaps one of the most picturesque sights of the many pleasing scenes on the island.

The Amphitheatre in connection with the Bathing Pavilion seats 2,000 persons, and overlooks the full extent of the Bathing Grounds. Concerts by Gilmore's band are given daily during the hours of 1 P. M. till 2:30, 3:30

until 4:30 P. M., and from 5 until 6 P. M. An admission of ten cents is charged to parties not needing baths, but it is free to bathers.

Several grand pyrotechnic displays by the Alexandra Company, of which Mr. Paine is at the head, will take place during the season, the grounds devoted to this purpose being at the east end of the Grand Pavilion.

At the back of the bathing houses will be seen the immense Amphitheatre, put up by the American Aeronautic Society, to enable the celebrated aeronaut, Professor Samuel King, to carry out his experiments and perfect his plans in the improvement of the art of aerial navigation. Having an outlook directly on the ocean, Mr. King can prosecute his experiments with a view of testing the practicability of a journey to Europe with advantage. He has two large balloons placed at his disposal, each containing 150,000 feet of gas, which is manufactured in an adjacent building, and the visitor will be accommodated with a seat in the gallery on paying twenty-five cents. Should he be desirous of traveling upward for a quarter of a mile, at the rate of three hundred feet a minute, this indulgence may be gratified upon application to the manager, upon the payment of a fee of five dollars. The would be aeronaut may undertake this feat with the greatest safety, as every part of the apparatus used has been tested and approved of by the best experts. The entire cost of buildings, apparatus, and balloon will reach nearly $50,000.

A drug store—the proprietor of which is Mr. Pyles of Fulton Avenue, Brooklyn—occupies the pavilion which did service as the music stand last season.

The railroad facilities are admirable; safety and comfort being paramount to any other consideration. The trains run frequently (see Time Table), and a journey by the way of East New York division, from the foot of Twenty-third Street, New York, does not occupy more than thirty-five minutes; and the excursionist who desires a delightful sail down the bay to Bay Ridge, L. I., will be well recompensed for the little extra time occupied by taking this route. Commodious steamers leave Twenty-second Street, North River, frequently during the day. On his arrival, the visitor can reach Brighton Beach by taking the Marine Railroad. This journey occupies but a few minutes—fare five cents.

BRIGHTON BEACH.

Our next stopping place will be Engeman's Bathing Pavilion, quite a large establishment. Before we attempt to mount the steps leading to it, we are accosted by a stout gentleman with the words "Try your strength, sir?—two blows for five cents." The would-be Samson avails himself of the heavy hammer placed in his hands, and, with a vigorous blow, tries to beat all previous records of other Samsons. The indicator denotes one hundred pounds as John's striking power, but he has perspired considerably in the attempt, together with the loss of a few stitches in his clothing. Nevertheless, an ambitious looker-on exclaims, "By George, if I can't beat that!" and leaving him in the act of divesting himself of his outer garments, we are attracted by a card announcing the exhibition of the smallest little people in the world. Should you have your good lady or sweetheart with you, she will naturally exclaim, "Now, dear, I have read so much about these little people that I will and must see them." "All right, deary, it will cost us twenty-five cents each. I don't begrudge the money, for they are the greatest curiosities of human nature." We enter the doors of the

MIDGETS' PALACE,

—(which, by the by, is situated at the east end of Engeman's Pavilion)—and we are introduced to General Mite; he is fifteen years of age, twenty-two inches high, and weighs only nine pounds. He is perfectly formed, intelligent, and handsome; and Lucia Zarate, who is sixteen years of age and weighs only four and three-quarters pounds, is a native of Mexico, and is the smallest lady in the world. Like most ladies, she is fond of talking, sprightly, addicted to dress, and very mischievous, and, although so tiny, is perfect in form. When the author avers that he can place this little lady in the pocket of his duster or coat, the reader will readily imagine how small she is. On exhibition with these are Admiral Dot and Jenny Quigley, both very small, but most attractive in manner. They are good vocalists and musicians, and their presence greatly adds to the success of this unique entertainment. After having wished the little ones good bye, and with our minds full of the wonderful freaks of nature, our

ears are now greeted with loud reports as from miniature cannon: these emanate from a shooting gallery in the rear of this exhibition under the management of Mr. Langcake, who has a number of rifles of the Remington, Weston, and Ballard patterns. The charge is ten cents for three shots. We now stroll through the piazza of the magnificent Bathing Pavilion known as

ENGEMAN'S.

The novel feature of this establishment is the new Bathing Bridge, which allows the bathers to enter and leave the water as clean as if they passed out of mid-ocean; it also protects them from the sun, and the timid can indulge in a bath, at high water, without leaving its sheltering arms.

This structure is a pleasing piece of architecture, and is one of the great improvements which have taken place on the Beach within the last few months. Attached to this Pavilion are Dining, Bar, and Billiard Rooms under first-class management. The rates of this establishment are reasonable. A little farther on we meet Crandall, the child's benefactor and the parent's tormentor. We shall probably find him with a baby in his arms, or adjusting a little one on a velocipede, of which he has quite a number on the beach. I believe Mr. Crandall will take care of children whilst the parents take a stroll or a bath; but Mr. Crandall must be careful who his patrons are; otherwise, by the end of the season, he may possibly be able to add to his establishment a miniature orphanage.

"Ah, Mr. Abrahams—(his stand is situated at the west end of the Pavilion), how do you do? How is the artistic business?" "First-rate, thank you, Sir; can't use my scissors fast enough." The gentleman addressed is a good artist in black and white. He cuts a facsimile of your portrait within a few minutes, by the aid of a pair of small shears. His charge is twenty-five cents for two pictures. The portrait engraved here was cut in the presence of the writer, and is a most excellent picture. At the back of this stand you can get weighed on Fairbanks' or somebody else's scales for five cents, and be presented with a record of your weight for future reference.

HOTEL BRIGHTON.

HOTEL BRIGHTON.

Here the excursionist will pause, and in wonder contemplate this magnificent block of buildings. He involuntarily exclaims: "What place is this?" Why, Brighton Beach Hotel, and the proprietors are Messrs. Breslin & Sweet, the former the well-known host of the Gilsey House, New York, and Willard's Hotel, Washington, and the latter the genial caterer of Fulton Street. It is difficult to describe the exact order of architecture of this building, but it reminds one of a picturesque Swiss structure with Gothic embellishments. From the long experience of the proprietors in hotel matters, it is hardly necessary to remark that all arrangements are perfect, and by the addition of a new wing to the building built this Spring, they are enabled to furnish two hundred and eighty guests with sleeping apartments. They have also restaurant facilities (under the management of Mr. Bliss of Brooklyn), for dining one thousand six hundred persons at one time. Here will be found both telegraph and railroad offices, and in the event of the weather becoming suddenly chilly, the hotel will immediately be heated by steam. The arrangements in case of fire are admirable. The hotel office is in charge of Messrs. Harris and Hitchcock, who through their uniform politeness and attention greatly add to the comforts of the tourist.

The Music Stand is simply a huge sounding board, built upon the most scientific principles, and the only one of the kind in this country. It is occupied by a band of forty musicians, under the leadership of Adolph Neuendorff, an accomplished musician, and well known from his association with the Philharmonic Society.

This hotel is situated at the terminus of the Brooklyn, Flatbush & Coney Island Railroad, one of the most popular routes of travel to and from the island, from the fact of its being central. It is under the superintendence of Mr. William E. Dorwin, to whose indefatigable and practical management the sole credit is due for the admirable manner in which this road has been conducted, both as regards time, safety, and convenience.

At the east end of this is the Drug Pavilion of Mr. Kitchen, of Brooklyn, —put up at a cost of $10,000. Within will be seen the great Centennial Soda-Water Fountain, exhibited by Mr. Tuft. A physician is in attendance here night and day.

At the back of Kitchen's will be seen the printing and publishing office of the *Coney Island Daily News*, a sprightly little paper devoted to the interests of the Island, price two cents. It has a large circulation. I may here remark that in addition there are also two weekly papers devoted to the interests of the island. One of them, *The Coney Island Herald*, is a New York enterprise, well and efficiently managed by New York journalists, issued weekly, and illustrated. It is an eight page sheet and published at one cent, and has a large circulation throughout the country. Its contemporary, the *Coney Island Sun*, also illustrated, is a first-class newspaper with a large circulation, published at one cent, and its many interesting articles will

B

be read with pleasure on the road or beach. These literary enterprises have been the means of drawing the public's attention to the various attractions of the beach, and they should be well supported by both residents and visitors. While speaking of newspapers, I may as well add that at Brighton Beach will be found the branch office the New York *Evening Telegram*, a paper with an immense circulation, which has been opened for the convenience of its subscribers. Advertisements are received here and the paper distributed at the same price as in New York.

Adjacent to this Hotel is the Ocean House. This is the oldest resort on Brighton Beach. Mr. W. A. Engeman is also the proprietor of this establishment. It has a clean, neat appearance, and is a good place to get a meal. It also offers excellent accommodation for driving parties. Situated immediately opposite this is a pier, also owned by the same gentleman, where the visitor can sit and inhale the cool and refreshing sea breeze without charge. Near this is the Brighton Beach Fair Ground, conducted under the same management. Here will be found amusements that will suit all tastes. It is a combination of a first-class Hippodrome and an admirable Race Course. A Grand Stand is now being built, to seat about 1,500 to 2,000 persons, and performances, or races, will continue every afternoon throughout the season. The Hippodrome is under the management of that veteran circus manager, Mr. Francis Whittaker, and the races are superintended by well-known sporting gentlemen.

We will cross the Concourse, and shall find a gentleman in green glasses. He has the largest galvanic battery ever exhibited. Ladies and gentlemen may be very much shocked or very little shocked for five cents, but Mr. Sackett is a good electrician, and will not overtax the nerves of his patrons. Next to him I find a humorous wizard, who undertakes to tell the fortunes of lovers, merchants, their sisters, their cousins, and their aunts, for ten cents. He has an arrangement, consisting of a stand and glass tube, within which is a little imp or devil, who, at the word of command, jumps from the infernal regions and writes your fortune. He stays in the land of bliss for a reasonable time, consistent with business, and an envelope is handed to you, perhaps containing a chromo of your intended. If we were all blessed with the good fortune he prophesies it would indeed be an ideal life.

We now continue our walk down the magnificent Concourse. It is nearly a mile in length, and both drive and walk are of a smooth, white surface of asphalt. It connects Brighton and West Brighton Beaches. Neat wagons are continually plying between the two places, the fare being five cents. We will here take a seat in one of the rustic cottages in the centre, and can also avail ourselves of the luxury of a drink of spring water from the fountain on the right or left. This is indeed a pleasing sight. Elegantly equipped carriages, liveried footmen, and their charming occupants in the shape of Brooklyn and New York belles and swells meet our wandering gaze. Now and then a dashing lady or gentleman rider passes us like a flash, and as we turn in our endeavor to follow the accomplished riders, we find that not a few prefer the ocean drive, for many are making their way to the Beach for a surf ride. I will here caution the excursionist with regard to this method of recreation. Not that there is any danger, unless the driver is worse than reckless, but the surf is so uncertain that it is hardly possible for you to get to your journey's end without a ducking. And I therefore advise the ladies to think of the pockets of their husbands and pa's before undertaking this feat ; and the husband to think that the spoiling of a suit of broadcloth, and having to replace it, may possibly deprive the dear one at home of the luxury of a new bonnet.

We now proceed, and pass a few pleasantly situated hotels, such as the Grand Central, Badens' and others. We cross to the right, and are attracted by a large crowd witnessing some performance going on in front of a neat building appropriately named the

NOVELTY THEATRE.

This theatre is under the proprietorship of Mr. W. F. Elliott, the well known Illusionist. Ladies and children need not hesitate to enter its doors, as all vulgarity is repudiated in its entertainments, which consist of balloon ascensions, tight rope walking, &c., in front of the building, with a concert on the balcony, in which Miss Burla, the celebrated Lady Cornet Soloist, takes part, while the laughter-producing farces, good singing, and dramatic entertainments within, will be the means of passing away many a pleasant hour. The price of admission is from ten to twenty-five cents. There are an hotel, dining and bar rooms attached to this theatre, giving excellent accommodation to a large number of guests, at perhaps the most reasonable charges on the island.

(SEE ILLUSTRATION ON NEXT PAGE.)

ELLIOTT'S NOVELTY THEATRE.

BRIGHTON BEACH.

We now retrace our steps back to the Concourse, and on the right pass an institution worthy of the support of every Christian. It is

THE SEA-SIDE HOME FOR CHILDREN.

If the reader will step in here and see the many sickly little ones trying to enjoy life in spite of the fearful ravages made in their constitutions from want of proper nourishment, and from the effect of long confinement in tenement houses, he will for a moment forget pleasure, and his hand will involuntarily be thrust into his pocket-book to give a trifle to assist a few more little children to the benefit of a day's holiday at the sea-

SEA-SIDE HOME FOR CHILDREN.

side. Here they have the best of food, while they inhale the invigorating ocean breeze. Supplied with a little shovel and pail they revel in the silver sand, while kind nurses occasionally give them a dip in the surf, strengthening their poor little limbs, and creating the merry laugh you so often hear among your own more favored little ones at home.

Having given your mite and wished God speed to the kind matron and her associates, we cross to the

SEA-SIDE AQUARIUM.

BRIGHTON BEACH.

SEA-SIDE AQUARIUM,

admission twenty-five cents, and well worth the money. Upon entering its doors the lover of natural history is greeted by the chattering of monkeys and the singing of birds, while odd, rare and beautiful fishes meet his gaze. Here is shown the baby hippopotamus (the behemoth of Scripture), the only one in this country. Then the visitor is gratified with a sight of that rare sea-monster, the white whale, who disports with the greatest ease—if not elegance, in the huge tank provided for his convenience. Mr. W. Conrad will exhibit the wonderful animal known as the cynocephalus. It is of African birth, and naturally very ferocious and wild, but with careful training has been taught to perform a number of astonishing tricks, only surpassed by that gentleman's wonderful performing dogs. Oscar's troupe of performing thoroughbred Kentucky horses also give two exhibitions daily. Their sagacity is wonderful, and the beholder can scarcely realize that he is simply witnessing the effects of proper training, and not the performance of animals endowed with reasoning powers. The whole of this large establishment is under the proprietorship of Messrs. Chas. Reiche and Brother, the proprietors of the New York Aquarium, who will add fresh novelties for the entertainment of their patrons during the season.

After leaving the Aquarium, we pass Thompson & Bennett's Hotel, one of the first established and most refined hotels on the island. It is run on the European plan, contains thirty rooms, is situated within one minute's walk from Culver's Depot, and its rates are from twelve to twenty dollars per week, according to location of rooms.

CABLE'S HOTEL.

WEST BRIGHTON BEACH.

We pass The Grand Union, a most excellent hotel with good accommodations, and Vandeveer's, the well-known Road House and Hotel, with good bathing accommodations near the beach, under the superintendence of Mrs. Vandeveer; but let me say a word for the little ones accompanying you; perhaps they would like a ride upon an elephant, a camel, a bear, or a donkey; if so, they can be accommodated by a worthy man opposite, and will be whirled round and round to their heart's delight to the tune of an accommodating organ, at a charge of ten cents. A low building on the right now meets our view—it is the depot of the

PROSPECT PARK AND CONEY ISLAND RAILROAD,

of which Mr. Audrew Culver is president, and Mr. Schemerhorn the efficient superintendent. In 1874 Mr. Culver built this road without any financial aid from other capitalists, and his enterprise and foresight, together with his indomitable pluck and perseverance, was, without a doubt, the means of inaugurating the idea of a Queen City by the Sea. How far this idea has been accomplished the reader will now be able to judge. Here we have no end of attraction. The railway facilities are first rate, every attention being paid to the comfort and safety of passengers; it is a pleasant route, and the excursion tickets are 25 cents. There is a branch line from here to "Norton's Point," which connects with the steamboats from New York. There are several stations on this line along the beach; the fare for the entire sea side journey is ten cents. (See Time Table.)

As we leave the depot our ears are greeted by the silver notes from the cornet of the world-renowned Arbuckle, who is engaged to give two concerts daily, with Downing's Ninth Regiment Band. Casting our eyes upwards, we are attracted by an immense but stately and picturesque piece of iron work. This is the

OBSERVATORY.

It is three hundred feet above the level of the sea, and a view of from thirty to fifty miles can be obtained, on a fine day. From this point the island and adjacent country have a most charming panoramic effect. The pleasure seekers below us appear like mere dots, and the palatial hotels, Manhattan and Brighton, appear like toy houses. Some of my readers will recognize this structure as the same as that put up at St. George's Hill,

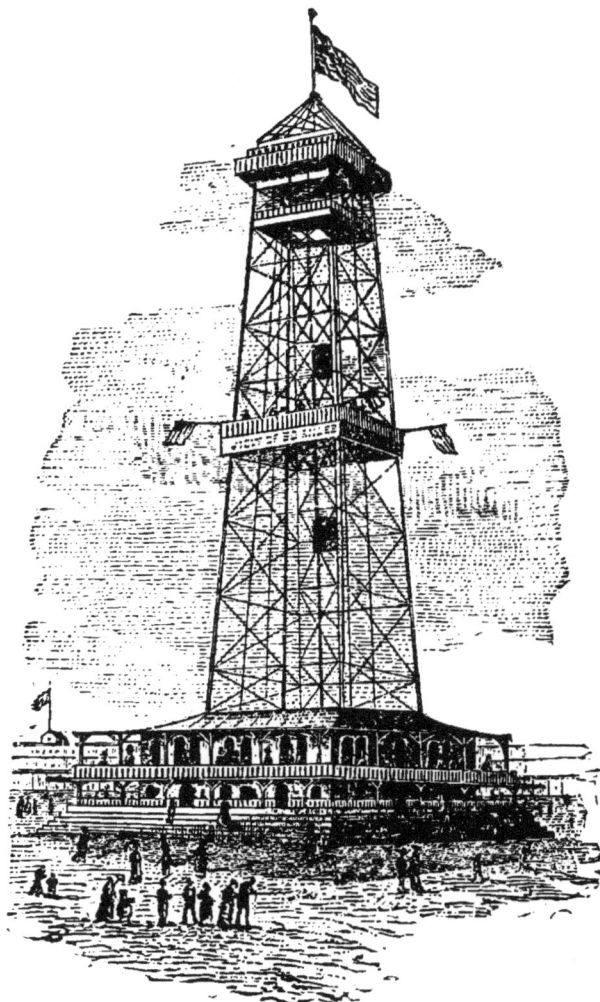

OBSERVATORY.

Philadelphia, during the Centennial year. It was transported at an enormous expense by Mr. Culver. After the several engineering difficulties of placing it firmly and securely in position, in a bed of sand, upon a foundation of solid brick (by no means an easy task), it stands up like a giant, a worthy monument to its proud possessors. The admission is fifteen cents. The journey upwards may be taken without fear, as the elevators are perfectly secure, for by means of a sliding bar the cars can be immediately stopped in their downward course, should any of the ropes break, which is almost an impossibility. It is under the management of J. L. Culver. Immediately between this and Cable's Hotel, is the wonderful

INTERIOR OF CAMERA OBSTURA.

WEST BRIGHTON BEACH.

CAMERA OBSCURA.

Some of my readers will ask the question, What is a Camera Obscura? It is simply a darkened room with mirrors placed in such a position in the roof that all surrounding objects within range of the mirrors are reflected by their aid on a white moveable disk below. Not only is the landscape or figures represented in their proper colors, but by this I may term it Nature's pencil; the motion of all objects are exquisitely rendered. The movements of even the leaves of the trees are seen, children charmingly dressed in various colors are seen to walk or run, horses and carriages move along, the argosies of our sea ports pass to and fro, the surf dashes on the beach, and the bathers are seen in their gambols; the clouds continually change as in nature, and the colors of the various objects are even more vivid (on account of the reduction in size) than in nature itself. The admission to the moving panorama is ten cents; Professor Janton is the proprietor.

As we are about leaving this unique exhibition, our attention is attracted by a middle-aged lady calling the attention of her spouse to a 'certain point in the picture, and exclaiming " Well, I never! what a shame, there's Mr. Black down here with Mrs. White; don't you see them together on the beach? What a wicked world this is." But the better half, more prudent in his remarks, calls the attention of the excited lady to the fact, that Mr. White is a few feet off giving his daughter Lillie a foot bath, in the most improved seaside fashion.

We now cross over a carpet of smoothly planed flooring and enter

CABLE'S HOTEL.

When Mr. Culver first opened his road he did not feel the necessity of building a pavilion, much less an hotel, but looked about for a large tent to protect the guests invited to the opening; not finding one to suit, he put up a pavilion, in which dinner was served. Soon after the need of a restaurant was too apparent, and, accordingly, the adjacent depot was built for this purpose and was occupied by Mr. T. E. Cable, the well known caterer, who has, since the building of the present structure, associated himself with Mr. Eastman, also well known as a practical hotel manager. The hotel is capable of providing rooms for 100 persons, and is for the accommodation of gentlemen only. Broad piazzas on the ground and second floors furnish facilities for feeding 6,000 persons daily.

The various attractions surrounding it, and the polite treatment of its guests by its genial manager, render it a favorite resort for bachelors. There are magnificent fountains of pure drinking water, innumerable and elegant lamps, which greatly enhance the beauties of the surroundings. The grand piazza, in front of the hotel and depot, is brilliantly illuminated, every night, by improved electric lights, equal to 25,000 candles, which produce the feeling of being in fairy land, rather than by the sea side. We re-cross the piazza and after passing Dr. Jackson's neat drug store, on the left, where the best of medicine may be obtained by those who unfortunately need it, and a little farther an elegant pavilion devoted to the sale of nic-nacks, cigars, and soda water, we cross over to

WEST BRIGHTON HOTEL.

WEST BRIGHTON BEACH.

BAUER'S WEST BRIGHTON HOTEL

formerly Atlantic Garden, and remark a large Pavilion with an immense cow. The lovers of pure milk will be interested in this poor animal; beautiful dairy maids milk her at the request of the visitor, and lo, and behold! milk as cold as ice is passed to their parched lips for five cents. Is not this a case for Mr. Bergh? For the proprietor is guilty of cruelty to animals—the poor cow was opened and a large refrigerator was placed in her body to contain the ice, above which gallons of milk are poured during the day, doing away with the necessity of a pump or well of spring water (rather difficult to be obtained on the Island); but the greatest outrage is that the authorities should allow this poor animal to be tortured by a mechanical contrivance by which milk is drawn by the same method as lager beer.

WEST BRIGHTON BEACH HOTEL,

formerly known as the Atlantic Garden, is under the proprietorship of the gentleman whose arrest I have advocated; but when you look at him full in the face, you cannot but come to the conclusion that he is a good fellow, and can hardly be guilty of the crime I have accused him of. His hotel is one of the most enjoyable places of resort on the beach, and is largely patronized, the accommodations being first class. There are one hundred well furnished rooms, and the restaurant is all that can be desired; the prices are reasonable, and it is almost impossible to take a meal without doing so regally, as music by the Red Hussar Band, with Bent Bros. as cornet soloists, will accompany you with every mouthful. Having satisfied our eating or drinking propensities, we travel on to the

NEW YORK AND OCEAN NAVIGATION COMPANY'S PIER.

This enormous structure is designated for promenading, bathing, eating, drinking, smoking, and for landing purposes. The admission is ten cents, either by landing from the boat or by the shore entrance. This great pier extends 1,200 feet into the ocean, and is built at right angles to the shore. Its width is 50 feet, with enlargements towards the pier head of 120, 83 and 100 feet. This structure has been erected upon strictly scientific principles, the engineers being Messrs. Maclay and Davies of New York, who assert that this huge piece of iron work, notwithstanding the continued shifting of the sand, will withstand the action of the most powerful surf, being elevated above the reach of storm waves. It rests upon wrought iron tubular piles, their cylindrical form insuring the greatest amount of strength. This Pier is well worth visiting. Almost immediately in the rear of this is the large depot of the

NEW YORK AND SEA BEACH RAILROAD.

It will be recognized as one of the Centennial buildings (the United States building). It has been re-built under the supervision of the well-known architect, Mr. Curtis, of New York. The president of this road is General

TILYOU'S HOTEL AND BATHING HOUSES.

LEACH'S WEST END PAVILION.

Ricker. The road is a wide gauge, double track, and connects with the steamboats at Bay Ridge at a point west of Culver's road. It is the largest terminus on the island, and it is the intention of the company during the next or following season to put up a hotel which will not only be attractive but will compete with the palatial buildings erected at the east end. The fare by this road will be fifty cents for an excursion ticket, including boat and rail. We now pass several bathing houses and restaurants, such as Feltman's and others, and meet a good-natured looking gentleman, with a slight rotundity of form. This is friend Dibble, the proprietor of the

WEST BRIGHTON PAVILION.

Here the visitor will receive a most hearty welcome. The inner man can be satisfied with roast or steamed clams, or any other sea-side luxury. There are about two hundred bath rooms attached to this establishment, one hundred being set aside for ladies, with dressing room attached. The prices are very moderate.

Proceeding on our journey we call at

TILYOU'S,

one of the quietest and most respectable family resorts at this end. This also is one of the first houses erected on the island. The proprietor is always anxious to comply with the wants of his guests. The *cuisine* is first-class, and the large number of bathing-houses, which are of a superior class, with faultless bathing apparel, had made the reputation of this establishment famous long before some of his more ambitious neighbors thought that an hotel would pay on the beach. The charges are reasonable. Near this we find

LEACH'S WEST END PAVILION.

This is also a well-known and respectable family resort. A good meal can always be obtained here at the most reasonable charges on the beach. Arrangements for bathing are first-class, and the surf here, as it generally is on this part of the island, is most enjoyable. Bathing suits are provided at the usual charge. In this locality there are several bathing-houses and saloons of small dimensions. We now arrive at a neat little building known as

GREASON'S NEWARK HOUSE.

Everything here will be found neat and clean. The restaurant is provided with all the delicacies of the season at the lowest rates. Polite waiters are always at hand to attend to the wants of its patrons. Attached to this house are a large number of new and improved bathing-houses of octagon shape, as shown in the sketch, and being new, no doubt they will be well patronized. The charge for room with bathing suit is twenty-five cents.

C *

GREASON'S NEWARK HOUSE.

Convenient to the Newark House, in the rear, is the depot of the

BROOKLYN, BATH AND CONEY ISLAND RAILROAD.

Mr. Charles Godfrey Gunther, the president of this road, must be admitted to be the leading pioneer of the Island. It was the first road constructed to carry passengers by steam to the beach, and was originally built for the accommodation of villagers living on this route. Had Mr. Gunther the foresight of others, there is no doubt he would have taken advantage of the many attractions this island was capable of developing. He unfortunately recognized this fact too late, otherwise this part of the Island would perhaps have been as attractive as Brighton or Manhattan Beach. But the future will tell a different story. The road is well managed, the cars are first class, neat and clean, and the trains connect at short intervals with the New York boats at Locust Grove. Single tickets, thirty cents; excursion tickets, fifty cents. (See Time Tables.) In connection with this depot is a large hotel, which has been named the Clarendon. It has been leased by Mr. B. Cohen, and contains forty rooms, newly furnished. Terms, including board, $10 to $15 a week.

We again pass several small buildings or pavilions, and are attracted by a neat pavilion or

PHOTOGRAPHIC GALLERY,

the proprietors of which are the well-known photographers of New York, Messrs. Speller & Eglotßtein. They are first-class artists, and their charges are very moderate. My friends, desiring to take home a sea-side picture of themselves to their wives or sweethearts, will do well to patronize them.

At the back of this pavilion will be seen one of the neatest hotels in appearance at this end of the beach; it is well conducted, with a good

WEST END.

PHOTOGRAPHIC GALLERY.

restaurant attached, and is favored with the name of a well-known New Yorker—it is

RAUCHER'S HOTEL.

Conveniently situated to the Brooklyn, Bath & Coney Island terminus, it has ninety bathing houses with double rooms, charge twenty-five cents, including bathing apparel. The bathing here is all that one can desire.

RAUCHER'S HOTEL AND PAVILION.

As we stroll along we notice several small buildings for bathing purposes, and stands devoted to the sale of fruit, milk, lemonade, cakes, etc., and notice on our right a neat little building known as

SMITH'S HOTEL.

Here will be found good bathing conveniences, and adjoining this is a neat structure called the Windsor (Laprovost's), well managed, with neatly furnished rooms for the accommodation of a large number of guests, at moderate charges. We are now getting to our journey's end, and as we pass we notice a fond mother giving her little ones a bath regardless of appearances, She has in her innocence adjusted her clothing the same as the little ones, and with her bare feet seems to enjoy the novelty of a sea-side foot bath as much as the little lambs whom she in her poverty is trying to entertain. A little further on we come across a gay party of revelers. I recognize them as being New York printers with their wives. One poor fellow, evidently with a weak back, is having himself sand-papered by his better-half by the aid of the pure sand, which she rubs in most vigorously, in spite of the laughter of the crowd. Their friends in the water seem to enjoy the fun. We will ask him why he goes through this painful operation. He answers cheerfully, "Why, sir, I've been suffering from rheumatism for years. The wife's soft hands and the silver sand open the pores of my ink-coated skin, and I'll feel a different man for the next month to come." We now reach the Rosedale Half-way House, occupied by Mr. J. B. McPherson, one of the oldest, and perhaps first settlers on the island. We pass and reach this gentleman's principal place of business, known as

WEST END.

POINT COMFORT HOUSE.

Rustic and cheerful, where all home comforts can be obtained, cleanliness here is paramount to godliness, and from the fact of his being an old resident the house is well known and appreciated. The surf here is delightful, no danger of undertows, the bathing suits provided for the use of guests are neat, and the two hundred bathing houses adjacent to the Hotel provide accommodation for all. There are several neatly furnished rooms for sleeping, and the house is easily reached either by Culver's Sea Beach Road or by steamer from Coney Island Point. We now finish our journey by arriving at

POINT COMFORT HOUSE.

WEST END.

NORTON AND MURRAY'S.

NORTON AND MURRAY'S,

And I think, after our five miles walk, we cannot do better than indulge in some kind of refreshment. The ladies no doubt will take soda water, the gentlemen, well, what ———, having quenched our parched throats and partaken of a substantial supper, we walk over to the beach, where the bathers are thoroughly enjoying themselves, keeping time to the excellent band provided for their entertainment, by the many funny antics they are cutting in the water. We notice the number of bathing houses along the beach to be about seven hundred, and these are well equipped. But, dear reader, I must now say good-bye, leaving you in the care of my friends, for like the ocean steamer just passing, I am homeward bound; I hear the shrill whistle of the boat at Norton's Landing which will land me in New York. Kindly remember me to your friends, but if I have not proved a GOOD AND EFFICIENT GUIDE, bury me in oblivion.

THE END.

OFFICIAL TIME TABLES

TO AND FROM CONEY ISLAND, BY RAIL OR BOAT, WITH FARES.

———•+•———

TO MANHATTAN BEACH.

Trains leave New York, foot of Twenty-third Street, crossing by Steamer Sylvan Grove.

A. M.—8.45, 9.45, 10.45, 11.15, 11.45.

P. M.—12.15, 12.45, 1.15, 1.45, 2.15, 2.45, 3.15, 3.45, 4.15, 4.45, 5.15, 5.45, 6.15, 6.45, 7.15, 7.45, 8.00, 8.15, 8.30, 9.00.

GREENPOINT DIVISION.

Leave, A. M.—6.30, 9.00, 10.00, 11.00, 12.00 M.

P. M.—12.30, 1.00, 1.30, 2.00, 2.30, 3.00, 3.30, 4.00, 4.30, 5.00, 5.30, 6.00, 6.30, 7.00, 7.30, 8.00, 8.30, 9.00.

Tickets may be obtained from the Long Island Railroad Company, at Flatbush and Bedford Aves., Brooklyn. Passengers take rapid transit via Atlantic Ave., making connection with the Manhattan Beach Railroad at East New York. Passengers taking the Grand or Roosevelt Street Ferries also connect at East New York by taking Broadway cars.

BAY RIDGE DIVISION.

Leave Twenty-second Street., N. R , via steamers Thomas Collyer, Twilight and D. R. Martin.

A. M.—9.10, 10.25, 11.25.

P. M.—12.25, 1.25, 2.25, 3.25, 4.25, 5.25. 6.25, 7.25, 8.25.

Leave Leroy St., N. R., A. M.—9.35, 10.35, 11.35.

P. M.—12.35, 1.35, 2.35, 3.35, 4.35, 5.35, 6.35.

Leave Pier 8, N. R., A. M.—9.55, 10.55, 11.55.

P. M.—12,55, 1,55, 2.55, 3,55, 4.55, 5.55, 6.55.

Leave Whitehall St., A. M.—9.25, 10.25, 11.25.

P. M.—1.25, 2.25, 3.25, 4.25, 5.25, 6.25, 7.25, 8.25.

The steamers Collyer and Twilight make alternate trips from Twenty-second St., Leroy St. and Pier 8. The D. R. Martin makes trips every hour from Whitehall St., Pier 1, E. R., adjacent to South Ferry, in connection with the elevated railways, but excursion tickets are not good except by the way of Bay Ridge.

OFFICIAL TIME TABLES.

FROM MANHATTAN BEACH TO GREENPOINT AND NEW YORK.

Leave, A. M.—7.35, 10.00, 11.05.

P. M.—12.05, 12.30, 1.10, 1.30, 2.15, 2.30, 3.15, 3.30, 4.15, 4.30, 5.15, 5.30, 6.15, 6.30, 7.15, 7.30, 8.15, 8.30, 9.00, 9.30, 10.35.

FROM MANHATTAN BEACH TO BAY RIDGE.

A. M.—8.10, 10.20, 11.20, 12.00 M.

P. M.—12.20, 1.00, 1.20, 2.00, 2.20, 3.00, 3.20, 4.00, 4.20, 5.00, 5.20, 6.00, 6.20, 7.00, 7.20, 8.00, 8.55, 9.20, 10.25.

Excursion tickets from New York, forty-five cents; single tickets, thirty-five cents. Excursion ticket from East New York, thirty-five cents, single tickets, twenty-five cents.

Arriving trains connect with the Marine Railway on Manhattan Beach for the convenience of passengers desiring to reach Brighton. The fare is five cents.

Last train leaves at 10.35 P. M., for Greenpoint and New York, and 10.25 for Bay Ridge.

These trains are equipped with palace cars.

BROOKLYN, FLATBUSH AND CONEY ISLAND RAILROAD VIA LONG ISLAND RAILROAD.

TO BRIGHTON BEACH.

Leave James Slip, New York, A. M.—8.30, 9.30, 10.30, 11.30.

P. M.—12.30, 1.30, 2.00, 2.30, 3.30, 4.30, 5.30, 6.30, 7.30, 8.00.

Leave Thirty-fourth Street, New York, A. M.—8.45, 9.45, 10.45, 11.45.

P. M.—12.45, 1.45, 2.15, 2.45, 3.45, 4.45, 5.45, 6.45, 7.45, 8.15.

Leave Hunter's Point, A. M.—9.00, 10.00, 11.00, 12.00 M.

P. M.—1.00, 2.00, 3.00, 4.00, 5.00, 6 00, 7.00, 8.00, 9.30.

Leave Flatbush Avenue, Brooklyn, A. M.—6.30, 7.30 (Sundays excepted), 8.30, 9.00, 9.30, 10.00, 10.30, 11.00, 11.30, 12.00 M.

P. M.—1.00, 1.30, 2.00, 2.30, 3.00, 3.30, 4.00, 4.30, 5.00, 5.30, 6.00, 6.30, 7.00, 7.30, 8.00, 8.30, 9.30, 10.00, 10.30, 11.00.

Leave Bedford Avenue, Brooklyn, A. M.—6.35, 7.35, 8.35, 9.05, 9.34, 10.17, 10.47, 11.17, 11.47.

P. M.—12.17, 12.47, 1.17, 1.47, 2.17, 2.47, 3.17, 3.47, 4.17, 4.47, 5.17, 5.47, 6.17, 6.47, 7.17, 7.47, 8.17, 8.47, 9.17, 9.47, 10.17, 11.04.

Leave Prospect Park, A. M.—6.40, 7.40, 8.40, 9.10, 9.39, 10.03, 10.22, 10.38, 10.52, 11.03, 11.22, 11.38, 11.52.

P. M.—12.08, 12.22, 12.38, 12.52, 1.08, 1.22, 1.38, 1.52, 2.08, 2.22, 2.38, 2.52, 3.08, 3.22, 3.38, 3.52, 4.08, 4.22, 4.38, 4.52, 5.08, 5.22, 5.38, 5.52, 6.08, 6.22, 6.38, 6.52, 7.08, 7.22, 7.38, 7.52, 8.08, 8.22, 8.38, 8.52, 9.08, 9.22, 9.38, 9.52, 10.08, 10.22, 10.38.

Take horse-cars to Flatbush Avenue from Fulton Ferry, or by Atlantic Avenue route from Fulton, Wall and South Ferries. Bedford Avenue Depot may be reached by Franklin Avenue cars from Grand or Roosevelt Street Ferries; also by Tompkins Avenue cars.

OFFICIAL TIME TABLES.

LEAVE BRIGHTON BEACH.

For Thirty-fourth Street Ferry, New York, A. M.—8.40, 11.15.

P. M.—12.40, 1.40, 2.40, 3.40, 4.40, 5.40, 6.40, 7.40, 8.40, 9.40, 10.10, 11.10.

For Flatbush Avenue, Brooklyn, A. M.—6.55, 7.55 (Sundays excepted), 8.25, 8.40, 9.26, 9.56, 10.26, 10.56, 11.26, 11.56.

P. M.—12.26, 1.26, 1.56, 2.26, 2.56, 3.26, 3.50, 4.26, 4.56, 5.50, 6.26, 6.56, 7.26, 7.56, 8.26, 8.56, 9.26, 9.56, 10.26, 11.00.

For Prospect Park, Bergen Street, and Bedford Station, A. M.—9.40, 10.10, 10.40, 11.16, 11.40.

P. M.—12.10, 12.42, 1.10, 1.42, 2.10, 2.42, 3.10, 3.42, 4.10, 4.42, 5.10, 5.42, 6.10, 6.42, 7.10, 7.42, 8.10, 8.42, 9.10, 9.42, 10.13.

Excursion ticket to or from Hunter's Point, 50 cents.
Excursion ticket to or from Flatbush Avenue, 45 cents.
Excursion ticket to or from Bedford Avenue, 40 cents.
Single ticket to Hunter's Point, 30 cents.
Single ticket to Flatbush Avenue, 25 cents.
Single ticket to Bedford Avenue, 20 cents.
These trains have Pullman Palace Cars attached.

Last Trains leave the Beach for Bedford Avenue at 10.33, for Flatbush Avenue at 11.00, and for Hunter's Point at 11.10 P. M.

PROSPECT PARK & CONEY ISLAND RAILROAD.

TO WEST BRIGHTON BEACH AND NORTON'S POINT.

Leave Greenwood, Ninth Avenue and Twentieth Street, Brooklyn—A. M.—6.30, 7.40, 9.00, 10.00, 10.30, 11.00, 11.30, 12.00 M.

P. M.—12.30, 1.00, 1.25, 1.45, 2.05, 2.20, 2.35, 2.55, 3.10, 3.25, 3.40, 4.00, 4.15, 4.30, 4.45, 5.05, 5.20, 5.35, 5.50, 6.10, 6.25, 6.40, 6.55, 7.15, 7.30, 7.45, 8.00, 8.20, 8.35, 8.50, 9.05, 9.25, 10.10, 10.30.

Leave West Brighton Beach for Greenwood—A. M.—7.05, 8.10, 9.30, 10.30, 11.00, 11.30, 12.00 M.

P. M.—12.30, 1.00, 1.25, 2.00, 2.35, 2.55, 3.10, 3.25, 3.40, 4.00, 4.15, 4.30, 4.45, 5.05, 5.20, 5.35, 5.50, 6.10, 6.25, 6.40, 6.55, 7.15, 7.30, 7.45, 8.00, 8.20, 8.35, 8.50, 9.05, 9.25, 9.40, 9.55, 10.10, 10.30, 10.45, 11.00.

Fare: Single Ticket, 20 cents; Excursion Ticket, 25 cents.

The following lines of horse cars connect with the above trains at Greenwood: Park and Vanderbilt Avenues, Adams Street and Fifth Avenue, Fifth Avenue via Furman Street, Jay, Smith and Ninth Streets, Hamilton Ferry and Ninth Street. Any of these cars may be reached from New York by Fulton, Catherine, Wall, South and Hamilton Ferries.

A branch of this road connects with steamers at Norton's Point, (see Steamboat Time Table.) Allow thirty minutes to make connections. Fare, 10 cents; excursion, 15 cents.

Last Train Leaves at 11.00 P. M.

NEW YORK AND SEA BEACH RAILROAD.

TO WEST BRIGHTON BEACH.

The steamers Morrisania and Sylvan Stream leave New York, connecting at Bay Ridge with trains for West Brighton Beach, as follows:

Twenty-second Street, N. R., A. M.—9.45, 10.45, 11.45.

P. M.—12.45, 1.45, 2.45, 3.45, 4.45, 5.45, 6.45, 7.45, 8.45.

Pier 43, Christopher Street, A. M.—9.55, 10.55, 11.55.

P. M.—12.55, 1.55, 2.55, 3.55, 4.55, 5.55, 6.55.   •

Pier 13, Cedar Street, A. M.—10.10, 11.10.

P: M.—12.10, 1.10, 2.10, 3.10, 4.10, 5.10, 6.10, 7.10.

Pier 1, Battery, A. M.—10.15, 11.15.

P. M.—12.15, 1.15, 2.15, 3.15, 4.15, 5.15, 7·15, 7.15.

Returning, leave West Brighton Beach for Bay Ridge and New York,

A. M.—8.00, 9.20, 10.20, 11.20.

P. M.—12.20, 1.20, †2.20, 3.20, 4.20, 5.20, 6.20, 7.20, *8.20, 9.30.

Trains marked thus * for Piers 1 and 13 only.

†Connecting with steamer Mary Powell.

Last Train Leaves 9.30 P. M.

HARLEM AND BAY RIDGE ROUTE.

The steamers Harlem and Shady Side leave Harlem (130th Street), connecting with trains at Bay Ridge, as follows:

A. M.—9.05, 10.10.

P. M.—1.15, 3.15, 4.15, 6.20.

Landing at 119th Street, Astoria, Greenpoint, Grand Street and Fulton Ferry.

Fulton Ferry Pier, A. M.—9.50, 11.00.

P. M.—2.20, 4.20, 5.20, 7.20.

Returning, leave West Brighton Beach, A. M.—10.20, 11.20.

P. M.—2.20, 4.20, 5.20, 7.20.

Excursion tickets, fifty cents. Single trip, thirty cents. Children, between 4 and 12 years of age, fifteen cents.

Last Boat Leaves at 7.20 P. M.

BROOKLYN, BATH AND CONEY ISLAND RAILROAD.

TO CONEY ISLAND.

Leave Greenwood, A. M.—6.20, 7.20, 8.10, 9.00, 9.50, 10.40, 11.30, 12.00 M.

P. M.—12.30, 1.00, 1.30, 2.00, 2.30, 3.00, 3.30, 4.00, 4.30. 5.00, 5.30, 6.00, 6.30, 7.00, 7.30, 8.20, 9.10, 9.30, 10.00, 11.00.

Returning, A. M.—7.30, 8.20, 9.10, 10.00, 10.50, 11.40.

P. M.—12.20, 1.20, 1.50, 2.20, 2.50, 3.20, 3.50, 4.20, 4.50, 5.20, 5.50, 6.20, 6.50, 7.20, 7.50, 8.20, 8.50, 9.20, 9.50, 10.20.

OFFICIAL TIME TABLES.

These trains connect with steamboats for New York at Locust Grove, arriving there eleven minutes later. (See Steamboat Time Table.)

Fare: Excursion Ticket, from Greenwood or New York via Locust Grove, fifty cents.

Last Train Leaves at 10.20 P. M.

HORSE CARS.—(SEE MAP.)

The Coney Island and Brooklyn Railroad Horse Cars run to and from the island half hourly, up to 11.00 P. M.; fare, excursion tickets fifteen cents. This line connects with all Greenwood cars.

STEAMBOATS,

WITH THEIR CONNECTIONS AND LANDING PLACES.

The steamers Rosedale, Idlewild, Chrystenah, Riverdale and Sylvan Dell, from New York, leave

West Twenty-fourth Street, A. M.—9.00, 10.00. 10.30, 11.00, 11.30, 12.00 M.
P. M.—1.00, 1.30, 2.00, 2.30, 3.00. 4.00, 5.00, 6.30, 7.30.

West Tenth Street, A. M.—9.10, 10.10, 10.40, 11.10, 11.40.
P. M.—12.10, 1.10, 1.40, 2.10, 2.40, 3.10, 4.10, 5.10, 6.40.

Franklin Street, A. M.—9.20, 10.20, 10.50, 11.20, 11.50.
P. M.—12.20, 1.20, 1.50, 2.20, 2.50, 3.20, 4.20, 5.20, 6.50.

Pier 2, A. M.—9.30, 10.30, 11.00, 11.30. 12.00 M.
P. M.—12.30, 1.30, 2.00, 2.30, 3.00, 3.30, 4.30, 5.30, 7.00.

Returning boats will leave Coney Island Point (now known as Norton's),

A. M.—10.10, 11.20, 11.50.
P. M.—12.20, 12.50, 1.20, 2.20, 3.20, 4.00, 4.30, 5.20, 6.30, 8.00, 10.00.

The 8.00 and 10.00 P. M. boats land at Franklin and West Twenty-fourth Streets only.

These boats connect with Culver's Beach Road. Fare : excursion ticket to Norton's, 40 cents—to Brighton via railroad, 50 cents ; single ticket to Norton's, 25 cents—to Brighton via railroad, 35 cents. Excursionists from Cable's will allow themselves at least thirty minutes to connect by train with the above boats.

Last Boat on this line from Norton's Landing Leaves at 10 P. M.

STEAMERS DIRECT TO THE TUBULAR PIER.

The steamers Americus, Minnie Cornell, J. B. Schuyler and Eliza Hancox, from New York, leave

West Twenty-second Street, A. M.—8.30, 9.15, 9.45, 10.45, 11.15.
P. M.—12.30, 1.15, 1.45, 2.15, 3.15, 3.45, 4.45, 5.15, 6.15, 8.00.

Leroy Street, A. M.—8.45, 9.30, 10.00, 11.00, 11.30.
P. M.—12.45, 1.30, 2.00, 2.30, 3.30, 4.00, 5.00, 5.30, 6.30, 8.15.

Pier 2, N. R., A. M.—9.00, 9.45, 10.15, 11.15, 11.45.
P. M.—1.00, 1.45, 2.15, 2.45, 3.45, 4.15, 5.15, 5.45, 6.45, 8.30.

OFFICIAL TIME TABLES.

Returning, leave Tubular Pier half-hourly up to 10.00 P. M.

Fare : single ticket, 35 cents ; excursion ticket, 50 cents ; which include admission to the Pier.   Return tickets are good on either boat.

The steamers Grand Republic and Columbia also make special excursions when the tide permits.

Last Boat Leaves at 10.00 P. M.

LOCUST GROVE ROUTE.

The saloon steamer Hampton leaves foot of Twenty-second Street, N. R., New York, 9.15 A. M., and 12.15 and 3.30 P. M; foot of Leroy Street, 9.25 A. M., 12.25 and 3.50 P. M. Pier 13, foot of Cedar Street, 9.35 A. M., 12.35 and 4 P. M., connecting with the trains of the Brooklyn, Bath & Coney Island R.R., leaving the Island at 11.15 A. M., 2.00 and 6. P. M.   Fare twenty-five cents ; excursion tickets, forty cents.

Last Boat Leaves at 6.00 P. M.

www.ingramcontent.com/pod-product-compliance
Lightning Source LLC
Chambersburg PA
CBHW021430090426
42739CB00009B/1424